WALKING IN YOUR PURPOSE
ONE DAY AT A TIME

WALKING IN YOUR PURPOSE: ONE DAY AT A TIME

SPIRITUAL AFFIRMATION BOOK 1

CHARMAINE HOLLAND

Roses
ARE
RED
PUBLISHING

ISBN-13: 978-1-955265-06-5

ISBN-10: 1-955265-06-2

Distributed by Roses Are Red Publishing

rosesareredpublishing.com

❀ Created with Vellum

BOOKS IN THE SPIRITUAL AFFIRMATION SERIES

Walking in Your Purpose: One day at a time

Walking With Grace: A life journey that never ends
(Coming soon!)

KEEP WALKING!

Dear Reader, thanks for reading. Let's stay in touch!

Visit me on my website at www.charmaineholland.com

Email me at hollandbook@gmail.com

Follow me on Facebook: https://www.facebook.com/charmainne.hollannd

Sign up for my newsletter, The Love of Inspiring Women here: http://eepurl.com/gGTV-P

Stepping into the Spiritual World of your Greatness

DEDICATION

*To my wonderful sons, who taught me so much about life,
including walking in my purpose.*

AUTHOR'S NOTE

I dedicate this book to my sons, Derek and Lloyd, for teaching me the principles of what parenting is all about. As I watched my sons mature into adulthood, I began to understand how powerful words can be to uplift and inspire, if they're used with the right intention and understanding.

Over the years, I developed an understanding of the importance of why we should listen more and talk less. If we become conscious of how we speak, we will experience more joy in life. To feel beautiful about ourselves and have the things we want in life, we must start to teach ourselves to speak highly with affirmations.

Creating this spiritual affirmations book has inspired me to share these words that I used to overcome my day-to-day life challenges. These affirmations have tremendously elevated my mind, body, and spirit. If you want a positive change that will develop growth in your life, these affirmations will definitely help inspire you to move forward in life.

Sending Love and Light Your Way,
  Charmaine Holland

INTRODUCTION

Walking In Your Purpose

Walking in your purpose. What does that really mean and how does one determine if they are walking in their purpose? We must begin the journey by removing any blockages that may be holding us back from moving forward —period. We must be honest with ourselves and identify any pain or hurtfulness that we are still holding onto. As we know, anything that is broken must go through a transformation period to receive healing. Healing strengthens the mind, body, and spirit into God's Glory of Greatness.

Healing the Mind, Body, and Soul

AFFIRMATION OF ACCEPTANCE

I respect the belief of others and strive to embrace the good in everyone.

Affirmation

- I accept my life the way it is.
- I see the beauty in every culture.
- I respect the beliefs of others and strive to embrace the good in everyone.
- I accept and love myself unconditionally.

ACCEPTANCE

W e must learn to accept ourselves before we ask or allow others to accept us. I recall this lady who was very nice and kind to people she met. She enjoyed supporting people and their events. This lady was trying to fit in so people would accept her and the gifts she brought. No matter how much she tried, though, she just couldn't fit in.

After years of pulling and pushing, the lady finally gave in and accepted God's plans for her life. At that point, she realized that God wanted her to stand alone and wait for people to come to her. This lady is now a motivational speaker about to travel all over the world to uplift and inspire millions of people. She learned to stand in her truth, living her purpose with affirmations.

AFFIRMATION OF BELIEF

I believe in everything I do that is in accordance with the will of the creator of the universe. My beliefs stand firm as I grow to be obedient to what I believe in and represent at all times.

Affirmation

- I am ready for anything.
- I will always love, respect, and believe in myself.
- Self-belief comes naturally to me.

BELIEF

Belief is knowing that you have the ability to do anything you set your mind to accomplish. Belief is having the heart to go through anything that God has prepared for you. Many of us grow up in life trying to make our parents happy by listening to their advice or suggestions, thinking it's best for us. I've learned that people's suggestions most of the time are best for them, rather than us. It's important to understand that we each have our own specific path in life that we must take to reach our purpose. Each path requires having the right tools to get us there. It's only our belief that will guide us to the right location.

AFFIRMATION OF COURAGE

Having the will and strength to overcome any obstacles in life gives us the courage to maintain our human dignity.

Affirmation

- I am strong and fearless.
- I am ready for anything that comes my way.
- I am brave and bold in my pursuit of happiness.

COURAGE

When we're little kids, our parents try to encourage us by teaching us to be motivated to do certain things that will enable us to gain strength to withstand adversity from a young age. If you notice, I started from the beginning, because this process continues to repeat itself over and over again with different situations throughout our lifetime. There's always something that we must strive to overcome in order to empower ourselves to be great. Without having courage at a young age, it definitely becomes challenging to master the difficulties that life brings us in our adult life. Therefore, we can appreciate and understand the lessons our parents were preparing us for before we begin to stand alone.

AFFIRMATION OF SELF-DOUBT

Doubt kills more dreams than failure ever will. Therefore, stay positive in everything you do to avoid doubting the possible.

Affirmation

- I forgive myself.
- I am more than enough.
- I am not defined by my past.
- I have learned many lessons and am fully equipped for better experiences.

SELF-DOUBT

Often in life, we come across the need for higher education to improve and test our skills. This is necessary whether we earn a degree or receive a certified license. As a life coach, I can recall throughout the years clients having self-doubt regarding many subjects; thinking they are just not enough. I don't know why we torture ourselves instead of expecting the best from ourselves. I do believe in time we will get better. I learned to always expect the best, especially when investing time and energy toward getting the best results that I expect, want, and deserve. So, yes, you will get through it and overcome anything over time!

AFFIRMATION OF SELF-ESTEEM

Self–Esteem indicates that within, you have the power and strength to make yourself happy without anyone coming into your life to do it for you!

Affirmation

- I am in charge of my happiness.
- I deserve good things in my life.
- I am worthy of having a great life.
- I am deserving of happiness, love, good health, and peace.

SELF-ESTEEM

Self-Esteem is an inside job, and that's a good thing, because only you have access to this place of power. An inside job requires self-work and gives you time to rebuild and restore any unfinished issues that may have been overlooked throughout the years. As you begin to strengthen your self-esteem, there will be times for assessment and re-evaluation to identify any existing issues. Healing can begin properly without allowing interference from others. While healing is happening, your self-esteem begins to elevate you to becoming a better person.

6

AFFIRMATION OF FEAR

Fear is an illusion of the mind and emotions. Once you face fear, it will automatically cease, and you'll be set free.

Affirmation

- I am capable of achieving anything.
- My future no longer frightens me.
- There are many good things happening in my life.

FEAR

Try this exercise:

Confront your fears by making a list of them. Then identify the why as you develop a solution to eliminate the notion.

I have come to realize that there are many kinds of fears holding us back. The fear of today is about overcoming obstacles in life and dealing with the uncertainties that living brings upon us. Many people fear losing their jobs, while others fear not getting the opportunity to have a job to pay and maintain household bills, mortgage or rent. There is also the fear of not having the proper health insurance or being able to pay for necessary medical expenses. Others who want to start a business experience fear, as they are unsure if they are capable of sustaining household expenses and other requirements. Some people are just afraid of making any changes, which constantly keeps them in fear of fully developing into their full potential in life. We must understand that fear only meets us when it's time for us to step outside our comfort zone. Fear is a reminder that it's time to take a leap of faith and make decisions immediately to move on with life.

AFFIRMATION OF GRATITUDE

Gratitude is having a mindset to appreciate the blessings that life offers us on a day-to-day basis.

Affirmation

- I am grateful for life itself.
- I am pleased to be present.
- I am grateful for the opportunities that life brings me.
- I am in awe of the beauty of life.

GRATITUDE

S howing gratitude is a form of expression that allows us to give thanks by being thankful and happy for the things that we have in life. Learning not to take things for granted allows us to see the beauty and importance that life can offer us in our lifetime. Being thankful has a way of releasing certain energy within us, making us always feel appreciative of life itself and what we have and what we know. Sometimes we get so busy with our daily lives that we overlook the small things that can make our lives so much easier. If we just stop and express our gratitude for things that we have now and what's to come, life can be so much easier for us in the future.

AFFIRMATION OF HEALING

Healing is identifying the pain and source that can heal your mental, physical, and emotional wounds.

Affirmation

- I am able to release and let go.
- I am in the process of healing.
- I will keep moving forward.
- I will stay positive about the idea of healing.

HEALING

Healing is the art of love. It takes time, it takes practice, and it takes patience. Finding love is a beautiful experience when someone loves you back unconditionally. Love is a universal energy force that's uncontrollable. Love is a cure for broken hearts and a healer of wounds. Now keep in mind, there's two kinds of love. One is spiritual love and the other is worldly love that we were taught. One deals with the intellect and the other deals with your heart. We should always have our arms open to embrace universal love at all times. But that's not the case for many people. When someone hurts you, it's not easy to bounce back for another dose of the unknown or uncertainties. I wish people truly understood the meaning behind love and where love actually comes from before giving or receiving it. Love is beautiful once you understand how to embrace love with the right mindset regarding receiving it.

AFFIRMATION OF INSECURITY

Having a mindset that you're not perfect or are incompetent will affect your thinking. That will bring upon insecurity issues.

Affirmation

- I love and accept myself as I am.
- I feel confident with my body, my job, and my life in general.
- I get along with people easily.
- I don't see other people's faults.
- I am aware and understand that no one is perfect.

INSECURITY

Being a single parent and not having the essential help and support to provide for one's household can make any parent feel a certain way about themselves. I have noticed how some single parents compare themselves to other parents who do have support. I can recall doing the same thing as a young, single mother and wishing I were like others. But I learned to take that energy and focus on myself, rather than others. When I began to focus on my strengths, I developed a solid strategy to provide the essentials that I needed to care for my family. Accomplishing certain things gave me the confidence and self-worth that I needed to overcome my insecurities in life and thrive as a single parent. This lesson has allowed me to stay focused on myself so I can achieve more in life, instead of comparing myself to others.

AFFIRMATION OF JEALOUSY

Jealousy can become a sickness of the heart that will hinder your soul, if you allow it. Avoid this emotion by showing gratitude and appreciating who you are.

Affirmation

- My feeling is valid, and I am learning what it means.
- My focus is on me and not others.
- I learned to replace my jealousy with serenity.
- Don't think about what might go wrong, think about what could go right.

JEALOUSY

What is jealousy? Jealousy is a disease of the heart that hinders our growth in life. This emotion keeps us from striving toward living our dreams. With jealousy, our focus is on watching others through their mirrors, instead of looking into our own mirrors. We must begin to admire our own qualities and gifts, which uplifts us and teaches us to appreciate our own self-worth. It's important that we identify and change what causes us to dislike something about ourselves before we look to others and begin to dislike them for what they have. Addressing the issue within ourselves releases the unpleasant feeling of jealousy.

AFFIRMATION OF KINDNESS

Kindness speaks volumes to your human existence.

Affirmation

- I always follow my natural instincts to be kind and thoughtful.
- I act with kindness.
- It feels good to be kind.
- I am mindful of other people and their feelings.

KINDNESS

Is kindness something that is taught or something that we learn along the way? Our parents teach us how to be polite and nice. But I think kindness is on a different level and entails an understanding of our feelings. There's a certain kind of love and compassion that we must carry within ourselves to demonstrate kindness. I realize it's not something we learn or develop overnight. It's a feeling that grows within us—that makes room for us to care about others as we care for ourselves. Kindness is an expression from the heart.

12

AFFIRMATION OF LOVE

Love is having the ability to express it, without expecting anything in return.

Affirmation

- I'm ready to give love so I can receive love.
- I am making room for an amazing partner in my life.
- I spread love to those around me to receive it in abundance.
- I am attracting love into my life.

To Love Yourself Affirmation

- I have the power to change my story.
- I am loved and lovable.
- I am worthy of a great relationship.
- I deserve love and affection.
- I am surrounded by love.

LOVE

What is Love? It's a powerful 4-letter word derived from the universe as energy. Love was designed to shape and form us into many different elements to help bring balance into our lives. If love is given with the right spirit and energy, one can feel uplifted, happy, and joyful at any given time. Sometimes the wrong energy can misuse the power of love and damage us emotionally, physically, and mentally. Love was designed for a spiritual purpose to take place from within to bring the best out of us at any given time through mind, body, and spirit.

CHAKRA AFFIRMATION

T his is a great tool to incorporate into your daily life routine. This exercise helps many women release blockages that are holding them back from moving forward in life.

Daily Chakra Affirmation

Root
Release Temptation
Let go of fear

Sacral
Honor Yourself
Have Confidence

Solar Plexus
Create Laughter
Let go of doubt

Heart
Accept Love Unconditionally
Give Yourself Love

Throat
Communicate your needs
Speak with confidence

3rd Eye
Be Mindful
Go with your first impression

Crown
To change a thought, you must change your view
Let Spirit guide your steps

KEEP WALKING INTO YOUR PURPOSE

As we begin to walk into our purpose, we will stumble greatly along the way. We will find many resting places to stop and ponder about what caused us to stumble. The moment we begin to accept and release by exhaling, we will build ourselves up with words of uplifting affirmation while reaching toward our greatness.

If you enjoyed the book, please leave a review on any book platform. If you don't have time to leave a review, please rate with stars. Every star helps!

THANK YOU

I thank you for your loving support!

Stepping into the Spiritual World of your Greatness

Www.theloveofinspiringwomen.com

ABOUT THE AUTHOR

Charmaine Holland's passion and love for humanity will sweep you off your feet. She is an intuitive life coach, healer and speaker, whose powerful, uplifting guidance has changed the lives of people all over the world.

For 30 years, Charmaine has taught people to seek their truth and live their best life by walking in their purpose and developing their true potential. Charmaine has worked with great spiritual leaders among communities for more than 20 years, helping establish healthy foundations of love within families.

Also an author, educator, financial advisor, and fashion designer, Charmaine is founder and president of four active businesses: Theloveofinspiringwomen.com, Ramadajournal.com, CharmaineHolland.com, and Hollandsbookkeeping.com. She is the proud mother of two great young men and six grandkids. Her family continually inspires her to leave the next generation a better future.

www.ingramcontent.com/pod-product-compliance
Lightning Source LLC
Chambersburg PA
CBHW072041060426
42449CB00010BA/2383